KNOWLEDGE

Wishing you the Very Best — a return to Knowledge ♥ Patricia

KNOWLEDGE

THE ESSENCE OF WORLD SCRIPTURES

PATRICIA ROBINETT

AESCULAPIUS PRESS
EUGENE, OREGON
2009

Aesculapius Press
Eugene, OR 97440-0256
Phone 541-484-0731
www.AesculapiusPress.com

Robinett, Patricia
Knowledge: The Essence of World Scriptures
ISBN 978-1-878411-20-4

1. Sacred books. 2. World scriptures. 3. Comparative religions.
4. Quotations. 5. Religion and spirituality

Most of the sources used here are in the public domain. Many of the quotes herein are composites,
gleaned from several different sources. Numerous dictionaries were consulted. Bible verses came
primarily from the King James Version (KJV), Young's Literal Translation, the New International
Version (noted with NIV®), as well as translations of the Bible from the Aramaic language
by Neil Douglas-Klotz, Rocco Errico, George Lamsa, Raphael Lataster and Vic Alexander.
Acknowledgment to The Message and the Amplified Bible. Sincerest thanks to all those who made
A Course In Miracles available.

Thanks to my friends who are always helpful in so many ways: Ava, Becky, Bruce, Carlotta,
Deidra, Emily, Hanny, Ib, Jesse, JoAnn, Kathy, Katie, Kristi, Lyn, Marilyn, Nan, Phyllis, Prem,
Richard, Rick, Scott, Tom, Wes

CONTENTMENT

It is needless to ask

of a saint the caste to which he belongs,

for the priest, the warrior.

the tradesman, and all the thirty-six castes,

alike are seeking for God.

It is folly to ask

what the caste of a saint may be.

The barber has sought God,

the washerwoman, and the carpenter —

Hindus and Muslims alike

have achieved that End,

where remains no mark of distinction.

Kabir

A LONG-FORGOTTEN LIGHT

THE LIGHT

Stirring from sleep with my eyes still closed, I was aware for one ecstatic moment of an ephemeral living light. It had no edges and it poured out of itself endlessly.

That was what I saw. What I felt in my heart was contentment, the fulfillment, peace and love I had always longed for.

On most dark, cold-to-the-bone, wintery Kansas City mornings Mama would flip on the electric light in the hallway, open my bedroom door and call out, "You're late for school!" in the hope, I suppose, of motivating me to jump out of the warm covers and move quickly. But this particular morning she came into the room and sat on my bed.

"What do you want for Christmas?" she asked.

I thought to myself, *I want to paint this light so I can remember it forever... but I dare not tell Mama. She will say, "Oh, Patricia, don't be silly! You're just imagining things!"*

Quietly, I said "Paints... paints and brushes and canvas."

THE PAINTS

Christmas morning, pleasant smells of turkey and mincemeat pie filled the kitchen, whereas my bedroom reeked of linseed oil and turpentine.

Sitting cross-legged on the floor, trying to capture the exquisite beauty of swirling layers of light moving over twirling layers of light whirling everywhere at once, but restricted to a small square piece of canvas stretched over a rigid board and thick, opaque oil paints, I did not experience much success.

Trying over and over again to capture the light of love, I applied paint and wiped it off, applied paint and wiped it off.

After several disheartening attempts, I gave up and made instead an honest self-portrait of a miserable teen, who for most of her life had wished to be dead.

That image filled the canvas — a white clown face with sad eyes, and under the big, bright red clown smile, a frown.

My misery was deep. All through my childhood a tender memory of pure, unconditional love had beckoned to me from long ago and far away and I *longed* for that love. For one moment in time, the light had come and love had at last filled the large, lonely, gaping, empty hole in my heart. It lingered a little while, but the memory eventually slipped away, and was forgotten for almost ten years.

From hindsight, I find it odd that not once did I ever connect my longing for pure love — or that beautiful inner light — to what religion referred to as "God".

Why is that? I wonder now. *Was it because the idea of "believing" kept me from thinking in terms of knowing God and receiving the gift of his presence?*

BELIEF

In Kansas — at least in the mid-1900s — God was something to *believe* in, not something to *know* or *feel*. God was also something to *fear* more than to *love*. If you didn't believe in God, the consequence was eternal punishment in an over-heated subterranean prison called *hell*, which was *hotter than Kansas in August,* supervised by a diabolical character who was *not* nice. He wore skintight red long winter underwear and carried a pitchfork with which he poked and prodded the unfortunate inhabitants of his fiery underworld — forever.

If you were not good, God would send you to that hell.

Believe in a punishing God and hell! Be afraid! Be very afraid!

Yet to be quite honest, belief had never been easy for me. By the age of three or four I had realized that there was no Easter Bunny, no Santa Claus and no Tooth Fairy. And now they were expecting me to believe in God?

SUNDAY SCHOOL

In a brightly sunlit classroom we children sang happily,

> *Jesus loves the little children...*
> *all the children of the world.*
> *Red and yellow, black and white...*
> *they are precious in his sight.*
> *Jesus loves the little children of the world!*

How wonderful this man Jesus must be! I asked the Sunday School teacher when he would be there because I wanted to meet him.

"Silly!" she said, "He died 2000 years ago!"

That night, laying awake in my bed, I couldn't get it out of my mind.

Two thousand years too late!

Tricked! I was tricked!

But then I heard a kind and gentle, measured, silent voice. It said, *Maybe something like that will happen during your lifetime.*

Ah, yes! I smiled, closed my eyes and slept peacefully.

CHURCH

Although the consequence for not believing in God was far worse than not believing in Santa Claus, the church said there was a loophole. If you had not lived a blameless life, you could ask for forgiveness just before you died and still get into heaven. But that didn't sound quite right to me.

There has to be more to it than that.

And so I found there *was* more to their theory... there was *memorization!* *Memorize Bible verses* and you might stand a better chance of pleasing God and getting to heaven. But memorization never felt quite right either.

And then there was *learning hymns* and *singing in the choir!* To be fair to the church, I remember my heart burst with joy whenever I sang the following song. This one felt right and good and true. I sang it with absolute sincerity and fortunately, we sang it rather often. It put into words my heart's deepest prayer.

> *Take my life and let it be,*
> *consecrated, Lord, to Thee...*
> *Take my moments and my days,*
> *let them flow in ceaseless praise...*

Then, at age twelve there was *confirmation:* a period of study, more memorization and more service to the church that culminated in a "coming of age" ceremony in which I was admitted as a full member of the Lutheran church. (A similar initiation occurs in Judaism and Catholicism.)

But if, as Teilhard de Chardin said, *Joy is the infallible sign of the presence of God,* then where was God that day? Our group photo shows only one happy face among nine confirmands... and my face was not the happy one.

As a teen, I began to seriously question whether I wanted to believe in a god who created people only to condemn them to hell for making mistakes. That concept completely clashed with what the Bible said: *God is love.*

Nor was I convinced that a minister named Reverend Rath (as sweet of a man as he was) could help me get out of my teenage hell of anger, rage, fury, grief and depression, let alone help me get to Heaven.

Eventually I decided there was no value for me in the church. Why belong to a social club, obey a bunch of rules to get to a heaven no one has seen, and — to top it off— profess blind belief in something that might turn out to be just another myth like the *Tooth Fairy?* Hearing about atheism, I liked the idea.

If there is no God, I figured, *then there is no need to worry about eternal punishment in Hell. So why not live it up?*

After college I put on my pair of ruby red slippers, moved to Los Angeles, and spent my early adult years doing just that.

THE SEARCH

At age 25, I found myself staying at the home of friends in western Kansas whose son had attended seminary. He had left behind a collection of theological books and so I read them all. By that time I was ready to learn more.

I had to be fair. How could I know for sure if God existed or not? So far "God" had only been a vague concept in my mind. Perhaps I would find something in these books I could finally believe, a good explanation of what God was.

Unfortunately, they contained nothing more than I'd heard before, but reading the book of Revelation in the Bible scared me to the marrow! If the Bible was true, then I thought perhaps it would be best for me to find out for sure, to stop living it up and *get with the program*.

I wanted to be one of the 144,000 who had *his Father's name written in their foreheads* — even though I had no idea what that meant at the time I read it.

I approached this new investigation with more passion and sincerity than I'd ever researched any subject before. And although I had forgotten that cold, dark, December morning, an angelic whisper deep inside said that I would have what I needed when I saw *light*.

A few months later, I was living and working south of San Francisco in what would someday be known as Silicon Valley. Weekdays were spent at IBM. Saturdays were spent at the East-West Bookshop in Menlo Park where I perused and purchased piles of books every week, hoping to find clues about the mysterious *light*.

To see *God's light* became my sole desire. It was all I wanted.

I avidly consumed volumes of world scriptures, devotional poetry, stories of saints, sages, mystics and masters, and contemporary reports of near-death experiences.

Some authors used the word *light* as a metaphor, to indicate an intellectual understanding or a vague good feeling, but that did not agree with my precious world scriptures. I wanted to see the beauty of the light the Upanishads described as *brighter than a thousand suns*.

Eventually I picked up the Bible again. By then I had developed a very acute sense of discernment and new life breathed its pages open to I John 1:5 where I read, *God is Light*.

Oh, my! That was *it!*

GOD IS LIGHT

Ah! I had read those three small words many times before, but this time they were fresh and bright and new.

God is Light flew off the page, bypassed my critical mind and landed right in the center of my heart.

God is Light. Something clicked. The words rang true.

Of this I was suddenly sure: John was not speaking metaphorically. He had *experienced* something. John had *seen* God and was saying that *God is,* quite literally, *Light!* And since John had seen God, that meant that I could see God too.

All the ancient books in my bookcase nodded in agreement.

Each one said, in essence, *What you are looking for is within you*.

I believed them.

Ask, they wisely advised, *and you will receive*.

Did I do it? Did I ask? Did I receive?

Well, not immediately, because I was stubbornly locked into a proud Midwestern do-it-yourself cowgirl kind of mindset — until I had *the dream*.

THE DREAM

I was at a school play rehearsal. My throat was tight with tears because I was homesick and I wanted more than anything to go home. But I wouldn't be allowed on the school bus without my books and looking around, I couldn't see them anywhere.

We were in the school gym and dozens of kids had thrown their books and coats into a big jumble on the floor, so I fell to my knees and began desperately digging through them. I'd pick up a book, look inside, and quickly throw it aside when I saw that it didn't have my name in it ... one book right after another ... until I reached the bottom of the pile and still hadn't found my books.

My head bowed for a good while. And, as things often happen in dreams, when I finally looked up, the pile of books had been replaced by my school locker — right there in the middle of the gym. Then I watched amazed as a hand reached around the locker from behind, lifted the latch and swung the door open wide.

There were my books! They'd been in my own locker all along!

A tremendous rush of relief surged through me.

WHAT DID THE DREAM MEAN?

Interpretation was easy, even for someone like me who was usually all thumbs when it came to decoding the language of dreams.

Shakespeare had written, *The world is but a play.*

Others speak of the world as a *school*.

I was clear that this world was not my real home because I'd been homesick my entire life, always crying inside, *Where is the love?* And now it was time for me to go home to where love was real, but I needed something first... I needed to *know* something, before I could go home.

Exhausting all the possibilities I was consciously aware of, all the books in libraries and bookstores, all the well-intentioned people who made promises they undoubtedly wanted to be able to keep but couldn't, I was bereft.

The dream said that what I needed to go home and to be at home, had been inside me all along: *The kingdom of God is within you.*

To that point the dream was simple and straightforward.

The shocker was the helping hand that had opened my locker door.

The possibility of receiving help was a radically new and different idea to me. Before this dream, I'd carried a life-long conviction that I had to do everything alone, all by myself.

No longer did I have to rigidly adhere to that limiting belief.

THE PRAYER

A few weeks later, my longing reached a point of desperation and found myself spontaneously following the Bible's advice, *Ask and you shall receive*.

My request was not made in the humblest or most graceful of fashions, but in an explosion of feeling. The words flew out before I could catch them, accentuated by pillow pounding at strategic points.

> *Damn it!* If *anybody's* ever seen you, *I* want to see you!
> If *anybody's* ever known you, *I* want to know you!
> If *anybody's* ever been with you, *I* want to be with you!
> *I'm your child too!*

Then I cringed and cowered and looked up fearfully toward the ceiling, fully expecting a lightning bolt to come crashing through! My heart of hearts knew that this prayer, as crude and as blunt as it was, would be answered. If nothing else, it was honest! My foot was in the door.

The lightning didn't come, but sleep did.

Eight hours later the wake-up timer system went off and muffled voices caught my attention. It was a radio talk show and the man who was being interviewed said something absolutely astonishing.

He had met someone who told him, *I can show you God*.

Needless to say, my eyes popped wide open and my ears perked up! Not wanting to miss another word, I wrapped myself in a blanket and crawled into the living room and sat cross-legged on the floor in front of the stereo.

If the radio voice had asked me to believe, I probably would have laughed aloud and turned it off. Instead, it continued, *"Don't* believe a word I say — *check it out for yourself."*

Is this a trick? I wondered.

The timing was altogether too perfect. First I had been told by my dream that help would come. Then, only eight hours ago I had prayed from the deepest place in my heart to see God, to know God. And now I hear that someone can show me exactly what I had asked for?

As if to clinch the deal, the interviewee concluded, "And if there's one chance in ten billion that it's true, you'd be a *fool* not to check it out."

Had the listening presence of God heard my prayer? Apparently so. And it let me know in a gentle way — no lightning bolts.

Yet this was a critical moment of faith and trust.

Shaking with excitement and hungry for some sort of affirmation, I picked up my Bible. As if by chance (and yet by this time I was beginning to suspect there was no such thing as coincidence) these wonderful words jumped off the page and into my eager eyes:

> *If a child asks for bread from any of you who is a father,*
> > *will you give him a stone?*
> *Or if he asks for a fish,*
> > *will you give him a serpent?*

I knew then that I would *not* be disappointed.

THIRTY-FIVE YEARS LATER

This book is the result of my 35-year love affair with the light inside. And just in case you are concerned that I might think I am special, fear not — I am very clear there is nothing special about *me*. What *is* special is the *light*. The light has always been there, is there now and will always be there — *in every one of us*.

Historically, knowing how to go within has been called *Knowledge*. The dictionary defines knowledge as "information and skills acquired through education; true, justified belief; awareness or familiarity based on experience."

Knowledge of the Lord is just that. It is a practical, dependable experience beyond opinion, belief, theology, religion, superstition or wishful thinking — once you learn how, from then on you know how to fill up on God, the love within you.

Everyone has occasionally dipped their toe in this lovely inner experience, as I did in my story above, and anyone who sincerely wants to learn how to enjoy it on a daily basis, can. It is our divine birthright and it is readily available. Millions of people around the world have received Knowledge: rich, poor, young, old, tall, small, educated or not. We can all know our true power.

Knowledge has been around for a very long time and has always been taught by the best of the best.

Once you have received it, you know forever afterwards how to go within. Yet it is always your choice whether or not to receive it and whether or not to use it. No one can ever take it away from you and no one can do it for you.

The day I received *Knowledge*, my face was radiant with joy, glowing from within — very different from my confirmation day photo. That day I learned that *light* was only one of several ways to connect with God.

MANY ROADS LEAD TO ROME

You may have heard people say, *Many roads lead to Rome*. It is true. We humans are endowed with a wealth of inner senses. Your outer physical senses are wonderful but they offer only a tiny hint of the majesty waiting for you inside. The inner experience far surpasses the outer. That is why the inner realm has been treasured and praised to the skies by so many for so long.

You can enjoy the kingdom within through the living light, inner music, divine love, and a delicious sweetness. The collection of quotes you hold in your hands makes it very clear that there is a vast storehouse of beauty that fulfills, satisfies and contents us like nothing in this world can.

Throughout the ages, people spoke about and wrote down glowing descriptions of *Knowledge* to share their joy with others because *Knowledge* was meant for everyone. *Knowledge* was openly celebrated.

Then came a dangerous political time in our own Judaic-Christian-Islamic tradition, when keepers of the sacred flame apparently felt it was necessary to hide their treasure — perhaps to preserve their lives. The leaders did not want a population that knew its spiritual power. To teach more secretly, some teachers then blurred and obscured the message.

In fact, when Jesus was asked by his disciples why he spoke to the general public in parables, he told them this:

The Knowledge of the secrets of the kingdom of heaven
has been given to you, but not to them.
Whoever has will be given more,
and he will have an abundance.
Whoever does not have,
even what he has will be taken from him.
This is why I speak to them in parables:
Though seeing, they do not see;
though hearing, they do not hear or understand.
In them is fulfilled the prophecy of Isaiah:

> *"You will be ever hearing but never understanding;*
> *you will be ever seeing but never perceiving.*
> *For this people's heart has become calloused;*
> *they hardly hear with their ears,*
> *and they have closed their eyes.*
> *Otherwise they might see with their eyes,*
> *hear with their ears, understand with their hearts*
> *and turn, and I would heal them."*

But blessed are your eyes because they see,
and your ears because they hear.
For I tell you the truth...
many prophets and righteous men
longed to see what you see but did not see it,
and to hear what you hear but did not hear it.

Matthew 13 NIV®

Today the earth is, as Isaiah said, *full of the Knowledge of the Lord as the waters cover the sea.* Since so many now know what is real and since we not only tolerate but celebrate diversity, coded language is no longer necessary. Therefore the quotes in this book contain the clearest descriptions of *Knowledge* that language allows.

However, there will always be challenges when writing and reading about something that lies beyond human concepts and language. As you read, please keep in mind:

- Languages change through time.
- Some translations are more accurate than others.
- Figures of speech, if taken literally, will confuse you.
- Literal descriptions, if taken symbolically, will do the same.
- The ephemeral quality of the subject matter is not easy to convey through words.

And since we are talking about something that cannot be measured in the external world, plus the language Jesus used was rich with metaphors, please carefully consider this wise counsel from *A Course In Miracles:*

All terms are potentially controversial and those who seek controversy will find it. Yet those who seek clarification will find it as well. They must, however, be willing to overlook controversy, recognizing that it is a defense against Truth in the form of a delaying maneuver.

Theological considerations as such are necessarily controversial, since they depend on belief and can therefore be accepted or rejected. A universal theology is impossible, but a universal experience is not only possible but necessary. It is this experience toward which the course is directed. Here alone consistency becomes possible because here alone uncertainty ends... Seek only this, and do not let theology delay you.

Please lay aside all your preconceived notions and assumptions, all your fears and doubts, everything you have been taught to think and believe, everything you've memorized, and read the verses in this book with the mind of a child: humble, open, eager to learn.

May you be blessed with the gift all scriptures praise.

They will neither harm nor destroy
in all my holy mountain,
for the earth shall be full
of the Knowledge of the Lord,
as the waters cover the sea.

Isaiah 11:9

DEDICATION

NINES & ONES

The number Americans dial when disaster strikes is 911 (nine-one-one). The date of the destruction of the twin towers in New York City was 9-11 (nine-eleven). The number nine with two ones has been linked in America with fear, destruction and violence.

With that in mind, please notice that the quote on the preceding page is Isaiah 11:9 (the opposite of 911), and the intention of the quote is to lead us away from fear, destruction and violence and to remind us of the profound inner *Knowledge of the Lord,* the subject of this book.

Therefore, this book is dedicated to Isaiah, whose words have long touched the hearts of all mankind...

It is dedicated to the masters and students from the past, whose words fill these pages...

And it is dedicated to Prem Rawat (also known as Maharaji) who kindly showed me 35 years ago how to see the light inside and who continues to inspire me still.

In the arena of knowing, he says, *there's no make-believe. You experience. It's not a fantasyland... You are here to experience Heaven.*

An international television program *Words of Peace* features talks by Prem Rawat, which can also be viewed on the web at www.WordsOfPeace.com and at www.Mspeaks.com.

QUESTIONS & ANSWERS

WHAT IS GOD?

WHO ARE YOU?

WHERE IS HEAVEN?

WHAT IS GOD?

God is Spirit;
and those who worship him
must worship in Spirit and in Truth.

John 4

God is Light;
in Him is no darkness at all.

1 John 1

God is Love;
who lives in love lives in God, and God in him.

I John 4

Moses said to God,

> *When I come to the children of Israel,*
> *and say to them,*
> *the God of your fathers has sent me to you*
> *and they ask me, What is His name? —*
> *what shall I tell them?*

God said to Moses,

> *Aheeyah ashara heeya…*
>> *Tell the sons of Israel,*
>> *Aheeyah has sent me to you.*

The Aramaic of The Peshitta

> *I am that which I am.*
>> *Say to the sons of Israel,*
>> *I Am has sent me to you.*

Young's Literal Translation

> *The living God.*
>> *I am the one who is.*
>> *I am the one who gives existence.*

Exodus 3

Hear, O Israel:
The Lord our God, the Lord is One.

Deuteronomy 6

God is One
and there is no other but him.

Mark 12

I am the Alpha and the Omega,
the beginning and end,
says the Lord,
that which is, and which was,
and which always will be.

Revelation 1

The recognition of God
is the recognition of yourself.
There is no separation
of God and His creation.

A Course In Miracles

"I am" is the Name of God…
God is none other than
the Self.

Sri Ramana Maharshi

The oneness of the Creator
and the creation
is your wholeness,
your sanity
and your limitless power.

A Course In Miracles

Everyone who loves
has been born of God
and knows God.
Whoever does not love
does not know God,
because God is Love.

I John 4 . NIV®

When you see Him
who was not born of woman,
throw yourselves down
upon your face
and worship Him…
He is your Father.

Gospel of Thomas

When God Himself reveals Himself,

He manifests that which can never be seen.

As the seed is in the plant and the shade is in the tree,

as the void is in the sky and infinite form is in the void —

from beyond the infinite, the infinite comes,

and from the infinite the finite extends.

The creature is in God, and God is in the creature.

They are ever distinct, yet ever one.

God Himself is the tree, the seed, and the germ,

the flower, the fruit, and the shade.

God Himself is the sun, the light,

and the lighted, creature, and creation.

God Himself is the manifest form, the infinite space,

the Breath, the Word, and the meaning.

God Himself is the limited and the limitless —

and beyond both the limited

and the limitless is He — pure being,

He is the immanent mind in Creator and creature.

The supreme soul is seen within the individual soul.

Kabir is blessed because he has this supreme vision.

Kabir

God is the Breath of all breath.

Kabir

The unreal never is — the Real is never not.
This Truth is known by those who can see the True.
The Eternal was never born and the Eternal never dies.
The Eternal is in Eternity: it is forevermore.
Never-born, eternal, beyond times past or to come,
Spirit does not die when the body dies.
Invisible to mortal eyes, beyond all thought and change.

Krishna

Something that cannot be defined

was whole and complete,

coming into existence before Heaven and Earth.

How still it was and formless,

standing alone, and never changing,

reaching everywhere, in constant motion

and yet in no danger of being exhausted!

You may think of it as the Mother of all things.

I do not know its name,

and so I call it the Tao, the Way or the Course.

Making further effort to give it a name I call it Great.

Great, it passes by in constant flow.

Passing by, it goes afar.

Having gone afar, it returns.

Therefore the Tao is great.

Man takes his law from the Earth;

the Earth takes its law from Heaven;

Heaven takes its law from the Tao.

The law of the Tao is its being what it is.

Lao Tsu

From the Invisible Whole
comes forth the visible whole.
And though the visible whole
has come out from
that Invisible Whole,
the Whole remains unaltered.

Isa-Upanishad

WHO ARE YOU?

Don't you know that you are the Temple of God
and that God's Spirit lives in you?
God's Temple is sacred,
and you are that Temple.

1 Corinthians 3

The Spirit of God moved over the face of the waters…
And God said,

> *Let us make man in our image, in our likeness.*
> *So God created man in His own image,*
> *in the image of God created He him;*
> *male and female created He them.*
> *And God saw every thing that He had made…*
> *and it was very good.*

Genesis 1

> *The Lord God formed man*
> *from the dust of the ground,*
> *and breathed into his nostrils*
> *the Breath of Life.*

Genesis 2

The Jews said to him,

      We are not stoning you for your good work,

      but for the blasphemy of calling yourself God.

Jesus answered them,

      Is it not written in your own scriptures:

      You are gods?

John 10

You are gods...
All of you are children of the most high.

Psalms 82

      When you know your Selves,

      then shall you be known,

      and you shall know that

      you are the Sons

      of the living Father.

The Gospel of Thomas

The sun and ocean are as nothing beside what you are.
The sunbeam sparkles only in the sunlight,
and the ripple dances as it rests upon the ocean.
Yet in neither sun nor ocean is the power that rests in you.

A Course In Miracles

I am blessed as a Son of God.

A Course In Miracles

You are the Holy Son of God Himself.

A Course In Miracles

The river and its waves are one.
Where is the difference
between the river and its waves?
When the wave rises, it is water —
and when it falls, it is the same water still.
Tell me, sir, where is the dividing line?
Once water has been called a wave,
is it no longer to be considered water?

Kabir

Who are you?

Who am I?

Where have I come from?

Who is my mother?

Who, my father?

Neither earth, nor water,

nor fire, nor air,

nor ether, nor sense-organ,

nor any combination of these, am I

because they all come and go.

That which remains

after taking away all else,

that auspicious Self I am.

The Self is extremely pure.

Shankaracharya

That thou art.

Shankaracharya

Know thy Self

Oracle at Delphi

In every heart there is pure Light…
that Light is what you are.

Sri Guru Granth Sahib

WHERE IS HEAVEN?

The coming of God's Kingdom
is not a matter of external observation.
People won't be able to say,
"Look, here it is!" or, "Look, there it is!" because
the Kingdom of God is within, inside of you.

Luke 17

Look to the Living One
for as long as you live.
Otherwise, when you die
and then try to see the Living One,
you will be unable to see.

Gospel of Thomas

Those who say that first they shall die
and then they shall arise are confused.
If they do not first receive the resurrection while they live,
they will not receive anything when they die.

Gospel of Philip

If those who lead you say,

"Behold, the Kingdom is in heaven,"

then the birds of the heaven will be before you.

If they say unto you,

"It is in the sea,"

then the fish will be before you.

But the Kingdom is within you, and it is outside of you.

The Gospel of Thomas

The Kingdom of Heaven
is the dwelling place of the Son of God,
who left not his Father and dwells not apart from Him.
Heaven is not a place nor a condition.
It is merely an awareness of perfect Oneness,
and the knowledge that there is nothing else;
nothing outside this Oneness, and nothing else within.

A Course In Miracles

Why wait for Heaven?
Those who seek the Light
are merely covering their eyes.
The Light is in them now.
Enlightenment is but a recognition,
not a change at all.

A Course In Miracles

Open the eye of Truth,
Discover the spiritual path.
Put your feet in the way of God
and seek his celestial court.
Once you have glimpsed that glory
you will no longer be attracted
to the tinsel and glitter of this world.

Farid ud-Din Attar

Within this earthen vessel
*   are gardens and groves,*
*   and within it is the Creator.*
*   Within this vessel*
*   are the seven seas*
*   and innumerable stars.*
*   And within this vessel*
*   the eternal sounds,*
*   and the spring wells up.*
*   Kabir says:*
*   Listen to me, my friend!*
*   My beloved Lord is within.*

Kabir

Where are you looking to find me?
I am closer than you imagine.
I am neither in temple nor in mosque,
neither in synagogue nor cathedral,
neither in rites nor rituals,
neither in yoga nor austerities.
If you are a true seeker,
you will see me immediately.
You will meet me in an instant. Kabir says,
God is the Breath of all breath.

Kabir

I laugh when I hear the fish in water is thirsty! Kabir

27

To look for Truth outside yourself
is to search for water outside of the ocean.

Toeong Seongcheol, Korean Buddhism

In the city of God is a secret dwelling place —
the lotus of the heart.
Within this dwelling is a space
and within that space
is the fulfillment of all desires.
The secret within that space
should be longed for,
actualized and realized.
As great as the infinite space beyond
is the infinite space within —
the lotus of the heart.
Heaven and earth are contained in that inner space —
fire and air,
sun and moon,
lightning and stars —
Everything is contained in that inner space.

Chandogya Upanishad

THE UNIVERSAL EXPERIENCE

YOUR INNER SENSES

LIGHT UPON LIGHT

THE SECRET SOUND OF SILENCE

THE FOOD THAT FEEDS YOUR EVERLASTING LIFE

HOLY SPIRIT, HOLY BREATH

WORD · NAME · TRUTH · WAY · LAW · TAO

YOUR INNER SENSES

I shall give you what no eye has seen,
what no ear has heard,
what no hand has touched
and what has never occurred to the human mind.

The Gospel of Thomas

The deaf will hear the words of a book,
and out of thick darkness,
the eyes of the blind do see.

Isaiah 29

Blind men see again, the lame walk, lepers are cleansed, the deaf hear, the dead are raised, and the destitute hear good news.

Luke 7

It is written:

The eye has not seen,

and the ear has not heard,

and the human heart cannot conceive

of those things God has prepared

for those who love Him.

But God has revealed them to us by His Spirit.

For the Spirit searches all things,

even into the very depths of God.

For who can know the mind of a man

except the spirit of the man himself?

In the same way,

no one can know the Mind of God

except the Spirit of God.

And we did not receive the spirit of the world,

but the Spirit that is from God,

so that we might have

Knowledge of God.

1 Corinthians 2

I love a certain kind of light and sound
and fragrance and food
and embrace in loving my God —
who is the light, sound, fragrance, food,
and embrace of my inner man…
where the light shines unto my soul
which no place can contain…
the sounds which time snatches not away,
a fragrance which no breeze disperses —
a food which no eating can diminish —
and a closeness which satiation cannot spoil.
This is what I love,
when I love my God.

Saint Augustine

The sight of Christ is all there is to see.

The song of Christ is all there is to hear.

The hand of Christ is all there is to hold.

There is no journey but to walk with Him.

A Course In Miracles

A universal theology is impossible,
but a universal experience
is not only possible but necessary.
Here alone uncertainty ends.

A Course In Miracles

Worldly senses are the ladder of earth
and spiritual senses are the ladder of heaven.

Rumi

My heart has five other senses of its own.

Rumi

The shadows of evening
fall thick and deep,
and the darkness of love
envelops the body and the mind.
Open the window to the west
and be lost in the sky of love.
Drink in the sweet honey
that steeps the petals
of the lotus of the heart.
Receive the waves in your body;
what splendor is in the region of the sea!
The sound of conches and bells are rising.
The Lord is in this vessel of my body.

Kabir

The thirst of the five senses is quenched there
and the three forms of misery are no more.

Kabir

39

The Tao eludes
the physical sense of sight —
it is invisible. It eludes
the physical sense of hearing —
it is inaudible. It eludes
the physical sense of touch —
it is intangible.
As the subtlety of the Tao cannot be grasped,
it may be thought of as a field of being.
Ceaseless and constant is its movement,
returning again and again to nothingness.
Form of the formless,
image of the imageless,
fleeting and ephemeral.
Were you to look before it,
you could not see its face;
were you to look behind it
you could not see its back...

All manifestations of motion
flow solely from the power of the Tao.
The Tao in itself is vague, impalpable —
how impalpable, how vague!
Yet within it there is form —
how vague, how impalpable!
And within that, there is substance.
How profound, how obscure!
Within all things is this unimaginable life force,
the quintessence of Reality, Truth.
From the beginning until now,
its Name has never passed away.
It watches over the creation of all things.
How did I learn all this?
From the Tao.

Lao Tsu

Too many colors blind the eye.
Too many sounds deafen the ear.
Too many flavors dull the tongue.
The wise turn from the outer illusion
and pursue the inner Reality.

Lao Tsu

It is the Ear of the ear,
the Mind of the mind,
the Symbol of the symbol,
the Breath of breath,
and the Eye of the eye.
Freed from the physical senses,
the wise become immortal.

Kena Upanishad

There is a well in the sky
from which Nectar is falling.
A lame man climbs up to it
and drinks his fill.
There are gongs ringing,
drums beating, cymbals clashing and trumpets sounding,
yet no one is playing them.
A deaf man listens to them and dances,
beside himself with joy.
There is a palace built where no world exists
and it shines with a brilliant Light day and night.
A blind man is overcome with joy simply to behold it.
There are living people who die
and are brought back to life again.
They are full of vitality,
yet they take no food.

Brahmanand Kavya

LIGHT UPON LIGHT

In everyone there is an eye of the soul
which is more precious by far
than ten thousand bodily eyes,
for by it alone is Truth perceived.

Plato

God is the Lord
who has shown us Light.

Psalms 118

Blessed are the pure in heart:
for they shall see God.

Matthew 5

Create in me
a pure heart, O God.

Psalms 51

And they shall see
His face.

Revelation 22

If thine eye be single,
thy whole body shall
be full of Light.

Matthew 6

If one is whole,
one will be filled with Light,
but if one is divided,
one will be filled with darkness.

Gospel of Thomas

Some who are standing here
will not taste death
before they see
the Kingdom of God.

Luke 9 . NIV®

Beyond the body,

beyond the sun and stars,

past everything you see and yet somehow familiar,

is an arc of golden Light

that stretches as you look into a great and shining circle.

And all the circle fills with Light before your eyes.

The edges of the circle disappear,

and what is in it is no longer contained at all.

The Light expands and covers everything,

extending to infinity

forever shining

and with no break or limit anywhere.

Within it everything is joined in perfect continuity.

Nor is it possible to imagine

that anything could be outside,

for there is nowhere that this Light is not.

And now the blind can see,

for that same song they sing in honor of their Creator

gives praise to them as well.

A Course In Miracles

Since my childhood
I have always seen a Light in my soul.
But not with the outer eyes
nor through the thoughts of my heart.
Neither do the five outer senses take part in this vision.
The Light I perceive is not of a local kind
but is much brighter than the cloud which bears the sun.
I cannot recognize any sort of form in this Light,
although I sometimes see in it another Light
that is known to me as the living Light.
While I am enjoying the spectacle of this Light
all sadness and sorrow vanish from my memory.

Saint Hildegarde of Bingen

He is the One
who sends His blessings on you
that He may bring you forth
out of utter darkness
into the Light.

Qur'an . Allies

Allah is the Light
of the heavens and the earth.
It is as if there were a niche
and within it a lamp —
the lamp enclosed in glass —
the glass a brilliant star lit from a blessed tree —
an olive, neither of the east nor of the west —
whose oil is well nigh luminous,
though no fire has touched it.
Light upon Light!
Allah guides to His Light
whom He will.

Qur'an . Light

Let reason go.

  For His Light burns reason up from head to toe.
If you wish to see that Face, seek another Eye.
  With two eyes you see double,
  And are unable to see the unity of the Truth.

Sa'd Ud Din Mahmud Shabistari

You have now realized
that there are two kinds of eyes:
an external and an internal…
that the former belongs to one world,
the world of senses
and that the internal vision
belongs to another world altogether,
the world of the realm celestial.

Al Ghazzali

51

He is the Sun of the Spirit, not of the sky.
  From his Light men and angels draw Life.
  That Sun is hidden inside the form of man.

Rumi

When you have accepted the Light, O beloved,
When you behold what is veiled without a veil,
  Like a star you will walk upon the heavens.

Rumi

Wash yourself of superficial personal identity,
that you may see your own deep, pure, bright essence!
Yes, see in your heart the pure Knowledge —
beyond book, beyond teacher or tutor.
The Prophet said, "He is one of my people,
who sees me with the same Light whereby I see him —
without traditions and scriptures and histories —
in the fount of the Water of Life."

Rumi

Do not go to the garden of flowers, O friend!
Do not go there —
In your body is a lush flower garden.
Sit upon the lotus of a thousand petals,
and gaze on the infinite beauty within.

Kabir

Look within and behold
how the moonbeams of the Secret One shine in you.
There, falls the rhythmic beat of life and death.
There, rapture wells forth
and all space is radiant with light…
There, millions of suns and moons are burning.
There, the drum beats and the lover swings in play.
Love songs resound.
Light rains down everywhere.
Drink deeply from the cup of heavenly nectar.
Look upon life and death —
there is no difference between them.
This Truth will never be found in books.

Kabir

The sun shines by day.
The moon illuminates the night.
A warrior with armor shines.
A brahmin shines in meditation.

Buddha

The man who
quietly undertakes
the way of perfection...
he sees Light.

Buddha

You cannot see me with human eyes...
I therefore give you divine sight.

Krishna

He is the Light of all lights

        shining beyond all darkness...

                dwelling in the hearts of all.

Krishna

The eyes that behold the Lord
are quite different from those
with which we see the world.

Guru Granth Sahib

The Primal One, the Pure Light,
without beginning, without end.
Throughout all the ages,
He is One and the Same.

Guru Nanak

57

The wise who strive
and who are pure
see Him within the body
in His pure glory and Light.

Mundaka Upanishad

There is a Light that shines
beyond all things on earth,
beyond us all,
beyond the heavens,
beyond the highest,
the very highest heavens.
This is the Light
that shines in your heart.

Chandogya Upanishad

Know this pure immortal Light…
know in Truth
this pure immortal Light.

Katha Upanishad

From the unreal,
lead me to the Real…
from darkness,
to Light…
and from death,
to Immortality.

Brihadaranyaka Upanishad

0 nobly-born,

the time has come for you to seek the path.

Your breathing is about to cease.

Your guru has set you face to face before

with the clear Light

and you are now about

to experience its Reality,

wherein all things are like

the empty, cloudless sky,

and the naked, spotless intellect

is like a transparent vacuum

without circumference or center.

At this moment, know your Self

and rest in that state.

0 nobly-born, listen.

Now you are experiencing the

radiance of the clear Light of pure Reality.

Recognize it.

0 nobly-born,

your present intellect —

its real nature empty, unformed,

without characteristics or color —

is the very Reality, the all-good.

Your own intellect, the Intellect itself,

unobstructed, shining, thrilling, and blissful,

is pure Consciousness, the all-good Buddha...

Your own Consciousness, not formed into anything...
and the Intellect, shining and blissful —
these two are inseparable.
Oneness is the state of perfect enlightenment.
Your own Consciousness,
shining, void, and inseparable
from the great body of radiance,
has neither birth, nor death,
and is the immutable Light.
Knowing this is sufficient.
Recognizing the voidness of your own intellect
to be Buddhahood,
and looking upon it
as being your own Consciousness,
is to keep yourself in a state of divine mind.
0 nobly-born,
when your body and mind were separating,
you must have caught
a glimpse of the pure Truth —
subtle, sparkling, bright, dazzling, glorious,
and radiantly awesome —
in appearance like a mirage
moving across a landscape in springtime
in one continuous stream of vibrations.
Be not daunted, nor terrified, nor awed.
That is the radiance of your own true Nature.
Recognize it.

8th Century Tibet . Tibetan Book of the Dead

A nature
which in the first place is
everlasting, not growing and decaying, or
waxing and waning; secondly, not fair in one point
of view and foul in another, or at one time or in one rela-
tion or at one place fair, at another time or in another relation
or at another place foul, as if fair to some and foul to others, or in the
likeness of a face or hands or any other part of the bodily frame, or in any
form of speech or knowledge, or existing in any other being, as for example, in
an animal, or in heaven or in earth, or in any other place; but beauty absolute,
separate, simple, and everlasting, which without diminution and without increase,
or any change, is imparted to the ever-growing and perishing beauties of all other
things. He who from these ascending under the influence of true love, begins to
perceive that beauty, is not far from the end ... he arrives at the notion of absolute
beauty, and at last knows what the essence of beauty is ... that life above all others
which man should live, in the contemplation of beauty absolute; a beauty which
if you once beheld, you would see not to be after the measure of gold, and gar-
ments... But what if man had eyes to see the true beauty — the divine beauty,
I mean, pure and dear and unalloyed, not clogged with the pollutions of
mortality and all the colors and vanities of human life? Remember
how in that communion only, beholding beauty with the eye of
the mind, he will be bringing forth and nourishing true
virtue to become the friend of God and
be immortal, if mortal man may.

Plato

They must lift the eye of the soul
to the universal Light
which lightens all things,
and behold the Absolute Good.

Plato

Who are the true philosophers?
Those who are lovers
of the Vision of Truth.

Plato

THE SECRET SOUND OF SILENCE

And behold, the Lord passed by
and a great and mighty wind tore the mountains,
and broke in pieces the rocks before the Lord,
but the Lord was not in the wind.
And after the wind an earthquake,
but the Lord was not in the earthquake.
And after the earthquake a fire,
but the Lord was not in the fire.
And after the fire…
a quiet whisper, a still, small voice.

1 Kings 19

There are melodies which require words.

That is the lowest degree.

There is also a higher degree:

    it is a melody that requires no words.

        It is sung without words, as a pure melody.

        But even this melody requires

        a voice and lips to express itself.

        The voice, though a nobler and higher form

        of matter, is still material in its essence.

        We may say that the voice is standing

        on the borderline between matter and spirit.

        Anyhow, the melody which is still dependent

        upon voice and lips is not yet pure,

        not yet entirely pure, not real spirit.

        The true, highest melody, however,

is that which is sung without any voice.

It resounds in the interior of man,

is vibrating in his heart and in all his limbs...

And that is how we are to understand
the words of King David,
> *when he says in his Psalms,*
>> *All my bones are praising the Lord.*
>> *The melody should vibrate*
>>> *in the marrow of our bones,*
>>>> *and such is the most beautiful song of praise*
>>>> *addressed to the Lord, blessed be His name.*
>>>> *For such a melody has not been invented*
>>>> *by a being of flesh and blood;*
>>>> *it is a portion of that melody with which*
>>>> *the Lord once created the Universe.*
>>> *It is a part of the soul*
which He has breathed into His creation
It is thus that the heavenly hosts are singing.

Rabbinic Literature . Reb Yekel

Blessed are the people
who know the joyful sound.
They shall walk, O Lord,
in the Light of your countenance.

Psalms 89

No one hears the song of Heaven
and remains without a voice
that adds its power to the song,
and makes it sweeter still.

A Course In Miracles

Listen to the secret Sound,
the real Sound, which is inside you.
The One no one talks of
speaks the secret Sound to Himself
and He is the One who has made it all.

Kabir

There comes a Sound
from neither within nor without,
from the place where the prophet Moses
saw the Divine Light.

Rumi

What concert is it
when the soul spins around,
dancing?

Rumi

Listen, — perhaps you catch a hint
of an ancient state not quite forgotten;
dim, perhaps, and yet not altogether unfamiliar,
like a song whose name is long forgotten,
and the circumstances in which you heard
completely unremembered.
Not the whole song has stayed with you,
but just a little wisp of melody,
attached not to a person or a place
or anything particular.
But you remember, from just this little part,
how lovely was the song,
how wonderful the setting where you heard it,
and how you loved those who were there
and listened with you...
The notes are nothing.
Yet you have kept them with you,
not for themselves, but as a soft reminder
of what would make you weep
if you remembered how dear it was to you.
You could remember, yet you are afraid,
believing you would lose the world
you learned since then.
And yet you know
that nothing in the world you learned
is half so dear as this.
Listen, and see if you remember an ancient song
you knew so long ago and held more dear
than any melody you taught yourself to cherish since.

A Course In Miracles

From within that Radiance,
the natural Sound of Reality
will come, reverberating like
a thousand simultaneous thunders.
That is the Sound
of your own true Self.
Be not daunted thereby,
nor terrified, nor awed.

Tibetan Book of the Dead

Hear again my Word supreme,
the secret Sound of silence.

Krishna

For insight, use your inner eye.
Use your inner ear
to pierce to the heart of things.

Taoist writings

Maybe you have heard
the music of man but not the music of earth.
Or you may have heard the music of earth
but you haven't heard the Music of Heaven.

Taoist writings

Who, by silence, can fill our inner Self with Music? *Lao Tsu*

What is the sound of one hand clapping? *Hakuin Ekaku*

Please play me a tune on a stringless harp. *Shuzan*

How sweetly enigmatic
is the transcendental sound…
a pure, subdued murmur
of the sea tide, setting inward.
The mysterious sound
of freedom and of peace.

Buddha

Sitting in solitude,
close the doors of the senses.
Concentrate your attention
on the subtle sounds of heavenly harmony.
Listen to the sweet sounds
of bells, conches, flutes
and stringed instruments.
Hear the beat of drums and the roar of thunder.
By listening to this harmony,
you become deeply absorbed
and the divine Sound appears.
All mental doubts and physical pains disappear.

Brahmanand Kavya

Bathe in the center of Sound
as in the endless flow of a waterfall...
listen to the Sound of sounds.

Vigyan Bhairava

The whole universe resounds with Sound
and you only need open the door of the ears.
To open the doors of the inner ear,
simply stop listening to external sounds.
Stay close to the melodious Sound
and lose yourself in it.
The supreme resides in a corner of your heart.
There is a glorious Music within you —
like bells, sitars and conch shells.

Sam Veda

Close the doors
of the three carnal senses:
eyes, ears and mouth.
Listen to the celestial Music attentively.
The mind will be absorbed in deep silence
and you will forget day and night.

Guru Granth Sahib

THE FOOD THAT FEEDS YOUR EVERLASTING LIFE

God is true.

His cup is pure.

Why should anyone who drinks Nectar

feel desire for mere wine?

I am intoxicated with the flow of Nectar.

Servant Nanak drinks in the ambrosial Nectar

and all his hunger and thirst are quenched.

Guru Nanak

And He humbled you,

and caused you to hunger and caused you to eat the Manna

(which you didn't know — even your fathers had not known),

in order to teach you that man does not live by bread alone,

but by every breath from the mouth of Jehovah man does live.

Deuteronomy 8

You may think you are looking for me

because you saw some miracles.

But you are really looking for me

because you ate the loaves and were fulfilled.

Do not work for food that spoils, but look for

the Food that feeds your Everlasting Life —

the Son of Man will give that to you.

God the Father has authorized him.

John 6

The Samaritan woman said to him,

> *You are a Jew and I am a Samaritan woman.*
>
> *How can you ask me for a drink?*
>
> *(For Jews do not associate with Samaritans.)*

Jesus answered her,

> *If you knew the gift of God*
>
> *and who it is that asks you for a drink,*
>
> *you would have asked him*
>
> *and he would have given you Living Water.*

Sir, the woman said,

> *You have nothing to draw with and the well is deep.*
>
> *Where can you get this living water?*
>
> *Are you greater than our father Jacob,*
>
> *who gave us the well and drank from it himself,*
>
> *as did also his sons and his flocks and herds?*

Jesus answered,

> *Everyone who drinks this water will be thirsty again,*
>
> *But anyone who drinks the Water I give shall never thirst…*
>
> *The Water I give becomes in him a well of Living Water,*
>
> *springing up into Everlasting Life.*

The woman said to him,

> *Sir, give me this water so that I won't get thirsty*
>
> *and have to keep coming here to draw water.*

John 4

To him who overcomes
will I give to eat
of the hidden Manna.

Revelations 2

I am the Alpha and Omega,
the beginning and the end.
I will give freely to the thirsty
from the fountain of the Water of Life.

Revelation 21

Experiencing the Truth and feasting upon it,

she passes down

into the interior of the heavens

and returns home.

There the charioteer

putting up his horses at the stall,

gives them

Ambrosia to eat and Nectar to drink.

Plato

I have shown you the way to the lake of Ambrosia,
which washes away all evil desire.
I have given you a refreshing drink, the awareness of Truth,
and he who drinks of it becomes
free from excitement, passion, and wrongdoing.

Buddha

My heart's bee drinks its Nectar.
Knowing it, the ignorant man becomes wise,
and the wise man becomes speechless and silent.
The worshipper is utterly inebriated.
His wisdom and his detachment are made perfect.
He drinks from the cup
of the inbreathings and the outbreathings of Love.
Dive into the Ocean of sweetness.
Let all concepts of life and death melt away.

Kabir

When at last you come
to the Ocean of happiness,
do not go back thirsty.
Drink the pure Water with every Breath.
Thirst for the Nectar.
Others have tasted it.
The saints are drunk with Love,
their thirst is for Love.

Kabir

My mind,
immersed in the Ocean
of the Nectar of Your Word,
has no desire to rise therefrom,
but craves for more and more.

Tantra of the Great Liberation

In the world of Brahman
there is a lake whose waters are like Nectar.
Whoever drinks there is straightway drunk with joy.
Beside the lake there is a tree
which yields the juice of Immortality

Chandogya Upanishad

HOLY SPIRIT, HOLY BREATH

I will ask the Father,

and he will give you another Counselor

to be with you forever…

the Spirit of Truth.

The world cannot accept him,

because it neither sees him nor knows him.

But you know him,

for he lives with you and is in you.

John 14 . NIV®

And the Spirit of God moved
over the face of the waters.
The Lord God sculpted man
from the dust of the ground,
breathed into his nostrils
the Breath of Life
and man became
a living being.

Genesis 1

God — who made the world and all things in it —
this One of heaven and earth, being Lord —
He neither lives in man-made temples,
nor is served by human hands.
It is not as if He needs anything,
since He gives all to all —
Life and Breath and all things.

Acts 17

He breathed on them,
and said to them,
Receive the Holy Spirit.

John 20 . NIV®

No one can enter
the Kingdom of God
without being born
of Water and of Spirit.
That which is born
of flesh is flesh
and that which is born
of Spirit is Spirit.
So don't be surprised
that I say,
You must be born again.
The wind blows
wherever it wishes.
And just as you can
hear its sound
but cannot tell
where it came from
or where it is going,
you also cannot explain
how people are born
of the Spirit.

John 3

If they ask you,

    "What is the sign of your Father in you?"

say to them,

    "It is movement and repose."

The Gospel of Thomas

What is it that always was
and had no beginning?
What is it that always is becoming
and yet never is?
The Lord of all moving things
is alone able to move of Himself.

Plato

This Breath of ours
by degrees steals back our souls
from the prison-house of earth.

Rumi

Between the poles of the conscious and the unconscious,
the mind has strung a swing.
On it hang all beings and all worlds.
That swing never ceases its sway.
Millions of beings are there.
The sun and the moon in their orbits are there.
Millions of ages pass.
And the swing moves on and on and on.
All are swinging! —
The sky and the earth and the air and the water
and the Lord Himself is taking form.

Kabir

When you give undivided attention to the Breath,
and follow it to a full and deep state of relaxation,
you will be as pure as a newborn baby.

Lao Tsu

Although the Tao, as it comes from the mouth
seems to have no substance or flavor,
and although it seems to be not worth
looking at or listening to — it is everything.

Lao Tsu

Ceaseless in its action,
it cannot be named,
and then it returns
and becomes nothing again.

Lao Tsu

Woven into his own creation,
Spirit is beyond destruction.
Never-born and eternal,
beyond times gone or to come,
No one can bring to an end
to Spirit which is everlasting,
beyond time. He dwells in bodies.
And although bodies have an end in time,
Spirit remains immeasurable, immortal.
Spirit does not die when the body dies.

Krishna

The Spirit in you is a river.

Its sacred bathing place is contemplation.

Its waters are Truth.

Its banks are holiness.

Its waters are Love.

Go to that river for purification.

Your soul cannot be made pure by mere water.

The Hitopadesa

Neither above, nor below, nor inside, nor outside,
nor in the middle, nor on either side,
nor in the eastern nor in the western direction am I.
Since I am all-pervading like ether,
I am indivisible by nature.
That one which remains after taking away all else,
that auspicious, absolute Self, I am.

Shankaracharya

WORD · NAME · TRUTH · WAY · LAW · TAO

The Tao that can be put into language
is not the eternal Tao.
The Name that can be spoken
is not the eternal Name.

Lao Tsu

Do not take the
Name of the Lord thy God
in vain.

Exodus 20

Your Word is revealed and all is Light.
It gives understanding even to the untaught.
I pant, I thirst, longing for your Law.
Turn to me and be gracious
as you have decreed for those who love your Name.
Rivers of tears run down my eyes
because men do not observe your Law.
Your Law is Truth.

Psalms 119

In the beginning was the Word,

and the Word was with God,

and the Word was God.

He was in the world,

and though the world was made by him,

the world did not know him.

He came to his own people,

and his own people did not accept him.

Yet to all who did accept him, to them

he gave the right to become Sons of God;

to those believing in his Name, who —

born not of blood, nor of a will of flesh,

nor of a human will,

but of God were born.

John 1

It is written:

Man does not live on bread alone, but on
every Word that comes from the mouth of God.

Matthew 4

Our Father which art in Heaven,
hallowed be thy Name.

Luke 11

I have revealed Your Name
to the men you gave to me.
They have kept Your Word.
Now they know that all things
you have given me came from you.

John 17

Sanctify them with the Truth —
your Word is Truth.

John 17

If you remain in my Word,
then you truly are my disciples,
and you will know the Truth,
and the Truth shall make you free.

John 8

*Grass withers and flowers fall,
but the Word of the Lord
endures forever.*

I Peter 1

*And His Name
is the
Word of God.*

Revelation 19

I will give him a white stone,
and in the stone is a new Name written,
known only to him who receives it.

Revelation 2

I have set before you an opened door
which no man can shut,
for you have shown strength
and have kept my Word
and have not denied my Name.

Revelation 3

How can I ever explain

that mysterious Word?

How can I say it is not like this,

and it is like that?

That Word makes

the inner and the outer worlds

indivisibly one.

The conscious and the unconscious —

both are its footstools.

It is neither manifest nor hidden.

It is neither revealed nor unrevealed.

There are no words

that can explain it.

Kabir

You, who seek no more of Him

than to name His Name?

What do His Name and fame suggest?

The idea of Him.

And the idea of Him

guides you to union with Him.

Rumi

Their faces are radiant;
the Music of the Essence,
the Word of God,
wells up within them.

Guru Nanak

Let the Word be the seed.
Irrigate it continually
with the water of Truth.
Become such a farmer,
and faith will sprout.
This brings Knowledge
of heaven and hell!
Do not think that your Lord
can be obtained by mere words.

Guru Nanak

What is meant by an eternally-abiding Reality?
The ancient road of Reality has been here all the time,
like gold, silver, or pearl preserved in the mine.
The Absolute Truth abides forever.
This Reality, this eternally-abiding Reality,
the self-regulating Reality, the Essence of things,
the Reality of things, the Truth itself.
There is just one Truth,
which has nothing to do with intellectualization.
The world seen as subject to discrimination
resembles a plantain tree, a dream, a mirage.
The realm of causation is perfect existence
and the highest Absolute.
The Essence, emptiness, Absolute Truth...
these I call Mind-only.

Lankavatara Sutra

That imperishable Word is the God of Light,

immortal in his glory, pure consciousness,

the Soul in all the Universe.

Svetasvatara Upanishad

The Way is beyond language,

for in it there is

no yesterday, no tomorrow, no today.

Chien-chih Seng-ts'an

PREPARATION OF THE HEART

PURIFICATION

DISCERNMENT

THE TEACHER

TRUST • SEEK • ASK • RECEIVE

PURIFICATION

Create in me a pure heart, O God,
and renew a right spirit within me.

Psalm 51

To the scorners
He gives scorn.
But to the humble
He gives compassion.

Proverbs 3

With pride
comes shame,
but with humility
comes wisdom.

Proverbs 11

Let the little children
come unto me,
and forbid them not
for of such
is the Kingdom of God.
Anyone who does not receive
the Kingdom of God
like a little child
will never enter it.

Luke 18

Blessed are the humble,

for theirs is the kingdom of heaven.

Blessed are the gentle and kind,

for they shall inherit the earth.

Blessed are those who hunger and thirst for Truth,

for they shall be well satisfied.

Blessed are the merciful,

for they shall have mercy.

Blessed are the pure in heart,

for they shall see God.

Blessed are the peacemakers,

for they shall be called Sons of God.

Matthew 5

If you do not turn
and become again
like little children,
you will never enter
the Kingdom of Heaven.
Whoever humbles himself
like this little child,
he is the greater
in the Kingdom of Heaven.

Matthew 18

Humility is a lesson for the ego,
not for the spirit.
Spirit is beyond humility,
because it recognizes its radiance
and gladly sheds its light everywhere.
The meek shall inherit the earth
because their egos are humble,
and this gives them truer perception.
The Kingdom of Heaven is the spirit's right,
whose beauty and dignity are far beyond doubt,
beyond perception, and stand forever
as the mark of the Love of God
for His creations,
who are wholly worthy of Him and only of Him.
Nothing else is sufficiently worthy to be a gift
for a creation of God Himself.

A Course In Miracles

Be humble before Him,
and yet great in Him.

A Course In Miracles

Humility will never ask that you remain content with littleness.
God did not create His dwelling place unworthy of Him.

A Course In Miracles

A dream of judgment came into the mind
that God created perfect as Himself.
And in that dream was Heaven changed to hell,
and God made enemy unto His Son.
How can God's Son awaken from the dream?
It is a dream of judgement.
So must he judge not, and he will waken.

A Course In Miracles

The holy instant does not come from your little willingness alone.

It is always the result of your small willingness

combined with the unlimited power of God's Will.

You have been wrong in thinking

that it is needful to prepare yourself for Him.

It is impossible to make arrogant preparations for holiness

and not believe that it is up to you

to establish the conditions for peace.

God has established them.

They do not wait upon your willingness for what they are.

Your willingness is needed

only to make it possible to teach you what they are.

A Course In Miracles

My Lord,

increase Knowledge unto me.

Qur'an . Ta Ha

You merely ask the question.

The answer is given.

Seek not to answer, but merely to receive the answer as it is given.

In preparing for the holy instant,

do not attempt to make yourself holy to be ready to receive it.

That is but to confuse your role with God's.

Purification is of God alone, and therefore for you.

Rather than seek to prepare yourself for Him, try to think thus:

I who am host to God am worthy of Him.

He Who established His dwelling place in me

created it as He would have it be.

It is not needful that I make it ready for Him,

but only that I do not interfere with His plan

to restore to me my own awareness of my readiness,

which is eternal.

I need add nothing to His plan.

But to receive it, I must be willing

not to substitute my own in place of it.

And that is all.

Add more, and you will merely take away the little that is asked.

A Course In Miracles

All things are magnets in the world.

The heat calls forth the heat, and cold the cold.

Foolishness fascinates the fools.

The well-directed pull the rest.

The fiery fuel those destined for hell.

The Luminous draw to themselves the Sons of Light.

The Pure attract the Immaculate,

while the melancholy are courting pain.

If you are miserable with your eyes closed,

it is because your eyes rejoice to see the daylight.

Keeping your eyes closed causes you grief —

they long to see the light of day.

If your eye is ever again troubling to you,

it is because you have closed your Heart's Eye!

Why not indulge your Heart's desire for Infinite Light?

When the absence of mere mundane earthly lights

distresses you, you open your eyes!

So, if separation from Eternal Light

brings you dismay — honor that!

Rumi

We shall be pure
and converse with other pure souls,
who know the clear light everywhere.
This Light is surely the Light of Truth,
because no impure thing
is allowed to approach the pure.

Socrates

Give up the notion,
"I am the body."

Shankaracharya

DISCERNMENT

The search for Truth
is simply the honest searching out
of everything that interferes with Truth.
Truth is.
It can neither be lost nor sought nor found.
It is there, wherever you are, being within you.
Yet it can be recognized or unrecognized, real or false to you.
If you hide it, it becomes unreal to you
because you hid it and surrounded it with fear.
Under each cornerstone of fear
on which you have erected
your insane system of belief,
the Truth lies hidden.

A Course In Miracles

Do not fear human disapproval
or be terrified by abusive insults.
For they will not last.
The moth and the worm
will devour them like woolen garments.
My righteousness will last forever,
my salvation through all generations.

Isaiah 51

Praise be to the Name of God
for ever and ever;
Wisdom and power are his.
He changes times and seasons;
he sets up kings and deposes them.
He gives Wisdom to the wise
and Knowledge to the discerning.
He reveals deep and hidden things;
he knows what hides in darkness,
and the Light dwells in him.

Daniel 2

Conform no longer to the ways of this world,
but let your mind be remade and
your nature be transformed.
You will be able to discern God's will for you
and to know what is good, pleasant and perfect.

Romans 12

Do not judge ... and you will not be judged.
Do not condemn ... and you will not be condemned.
Forgive ... and you will be forgiven.

Luke 6

Here in this holy place
does Truth stand waiting to receive you in silent blessing,
and in peace so real and so encompassing
that nothing stands outside.
Leave all illusions of yourself outside this place,
to which you come in hope and honesty.

A Course In Miracles

Be abstinent.
Abstain from vague thoughts.
There are lions in the desert of thoughts.
Abstinence is the prince of medicines,
As scratching only aggravates a scab.
Abstinence is certainly the root of medicine;
Practise abstinence, see how it invigorates thy soul!
Abstain from vague thoughts.

Rumi

Discern form from substance,
as lion from desert sands,
or as sound and speech
from the thoughts they convey.
Sound and speech arise from thought.
And even though you cannot see the Ocean of Thought,
when you hear the sweet waves of speech
you know a glorious Ocean surges beneath them.
Waves of thought arise from the Ocean of Wisdom.
They assume the forms of sound and speech.
These forms are born and die again —
they cast themselves back into the Ocean.
Form is born of that which is formless,
for "Verily to Him do we return."

Rumi

THE TEACHER

The ancient masters
penetrated the deepest mysteries of the Tao.
They were wise enough
to avoid most people's knowledge.
Their Knowledge
was beyond human knowledge.

Lao Tsu

Let your house be a meeting place for the wise.

Get sooty with the dust of their feet.

Drink their words thirstily.

Mishnah, Avot 1

Who is wise?

Stay close to him.

Prepare to listen to every story,

do not let his wise words escape you.

If you find an intelligent man,

visit him early;

let your foot wear out his doorstep.

Sirach 6

When Jesus had washed their feet,

and taken his garments, and resumed his place,

he said to them,

Do you know what I have done to you?

You call me Teacher and Lord;

and you are right, for so I am.

If I then, your Lord and Teacher,

have washed your feet,

you also ought to wash one another's feet.

For I have given you an example,

that you also should do

as I have done to you.

A servant is not greater than his master;

nor is he who is sent greater than he who sent him.

If you know these things,

blessed are you if you do them.

John 13

Humility is strength
in this sense only;
that to recognise and accept
the fact that you do not know
is to recognise and accept
the fact that He does know.

A Course In Miracles

Awe should be reserved for revelation,

to which it is perfectly and correctly applicable.

It is not appropriate for miracles

because a state of awe is worshipful,

implying that one of a lesser order

stands before his Creator.

You are a perfect creation,

and should experience awe

only in the presence of the Creator of perfection.

The miracle is therefore a sign of love among equals.

Equals should not be in awe of one another

because awe implies inequality.

It is therefore an inappropriate reaction to me.

An elder brother is entitled to respect

for his greater experience,

and obedience for his greater wisdom.

He is also entitled to love

because he is a brother,

and to devotion if he is devoted.

It is only my devotion that entitles me to yours.

There is nothing about me that you cannot attain.

A Course In Miracles

Approach someone who has realized the purpose of life
and question him with reverence and devotion.
He will instruct you in this Wisdom.
Once you attain it, you will never be deluded.
You will see all creatures in the Self, and all in Me.

Krishna

To a pupil who comes
with mind and senses in peace,
the teacher gives the vision of
the Spirit of Truth and eternity.

Mundaka Upanishad

Ask your teachers
to know that thing by which
the ears hear,
the mind thinks and
the unknown is known.

Chandogya Upanishad

To many it is not given to hear of the Self.

Many, though they hear of it, do not understand it.

Wonderful is he who speaks of it.

Intelligent is he who learns of it.

Blessed is he who, taught by a good teacher,

is able to understand it.

The Truth of the Self cannot be fully understood

when taught by an ignorant man,

for opinions regarding it,

not founded in Knowledge,

vary one from another.

Subtler than the subtlest is this Self, and beyond all logic.

Taught by a teacher who knows the Self and Brahman as one,

a man leaves vain theory behind and attains to Truth.

The awakening which you have known

does not come through the intellect,

but rather, in fullest measure, from the lips of the wise....

Words cannot reveal him.

Mind cannot reach him.

Eyes do not see him.

How then can he be understood,

other than when taught by those seers

who indeed have known him?

Katha Upanishad

*There is nothing in all
the three worlds that can be compared
to the True Teacher who imparts the Knowledge of
the Self. The legendary philosopher's stone may perhaps
be suggested as an apt comparison, because it has the capac-
ity to convert a piece of iron into gold, just as the True Teacher
converts an ordinary disciple into an enlightened person. But this
comparison cannot stand because, while the True Teacher makes the
disciple another Teacher like himself, the Philosopher's stone does not
have the power to convert a piece of iron into another Philosopher's
stone like itself. Therefore the True Teacher is incomparable and
even transcends the world in glory.*

Shankaracharya

I bow down to my most adorable Teacher
who is all-knowing and has,
by imparting Knowledge to us,
saved us from an endless ocean
of births and deaths,
filled with ignorance

Shankaracharya

Your teacher lives in eternal bliss
even now,
while he is still in the body.
He has come to teach you
how to have as much
peace and happiness
as he has.

Buddha

My teaching is pure.
It does not discriminate between
noble and humble, rich and poor.
It is like water —
cleansing all things without distinction.
It is like fire —
consuming all things, great and small.
It is like the heavens,
for there is room in it — ample room —
to receive all men and women,
boys and girls, the powerful and the lowly.

Buddha

One not knowing a land

asks of one who knows it,

he goes forward

instructed by the knowing one.

Such, indeed, is the blessing of instruction,

one finds a path that leads him straight onward.

Rig Veda

If a person has a sincere fervor for the Lord

and is eager to follow a spiritual path,

he is sure to meet a true Teacher

through the grace of the Lord.

Consequently, the spiritual aspirant

should not be troubled

about the coming of a Teacher.

Brahmananda

TRUST · SEEK · ASK · RECEIVE

Everyone who asks, receives.

He who seeks, finds.

And for he who knocks, it shall be opened.

If you are a father and your son asks for bread,

will you give him a stone?

If he asks for a fish, will you give him a snake?

Or if he asks for an egg, will you give him a scorpion?

You are decent to your children.

So know that when you ask for the Holy Spirit,

your loving Father will give it to you.

Luke 11

God is not a man, that he should lie.

Neither is he a son of man,

who changes his mind.

Has he ever spoken and then not acted?

Has he ever made a promise and not fulfilled it?

I have received a command to bless —

he has blessed —

and I cannot change that.

Numbers 23

If you seek the Lord your God
with all your heart
and with all your soul
you will find him.

Deuteronomy 4

I love those who love me.
And those who seek me, find me.

Proverbs 8

141

Ask, and it shall be given to you.
Seek, and you shall find.
Knock, and it shall be opened for you.
For everyone who is asking, does receive.
Everyone who is seeking, does find.
And for everyone who is knocking,
it shall be opened.

Luke 11

Fear not, little flock;
for it is your Father's good pleasure
to give you the Kingdom.

Luke 12

Be joyful always.
Pray without ceasing.
In everything give thanks.

1 Thessalonians 5

Ask and it shall be given you,
because it has already been given.
Ask for light and learn that you are light.

A Course In Miracles

Don't be so concerned about your life —

what you will eat and drink —

what you will wear on your body.

Isn't life more than food,

and the body more than clothing?

Look at the birds in the air —

they neither sow nor reap, nor store food,

and your heavenly Father feeds them.

Aren't you even more precious than they are?

Can you, by worrying, add an hour to your life?

An inch to your height?

And why do you worry about clothes?

Look at the lilies in the meadow.

They don't work or spin...

and yet not even Solomon in all his glory

was dressed as beautifully as one small flower.

Don't ask, "What will we eat?" or,

"What will we drink?" or, "What will we wear?"

for your heavenly Father knows all your needs...

Instead, Seek first His kingdom and His righteousness...

And all these things will be given to you as well.

Matthew 6

There is nothing concealed,
that shall not be revealed;
and nothing hidden
that shall not be known.

Matthew 10

I am very near.
I answer the call of him who calls,
when he calls to me.

Qur'an . The Cow

Who is saying a prayer to Me
that I may answer it?
Who is asking something of Me
that I may give it him?
Who is asking forgiveness of Me
that I may forgive him?

Hadith Qudsi

Why so impatient, my heart?
He who watches over birds, beasts, and insects,
He who cared for you
while you were still forming in your mother's womb,
Shall He not care for you now that you've been born?

Kabir

The Great Spirit is everywhere.
He hears whatever is in
our minds and hearts.

Native American . Black Elk

THE GIFTS

KNOWLEDGE

LOVE & JOY

FREEDOM FROM FEAR

PEACE

KNOWLEDGE

Tune your ear to wisdom.
Set your heart on a life of understanding,
Cry for Knowledge and call out for inner sight.
Look for Knowledge as if you are mining for silver.
Search for it as if you are digging for buried treasure.
Then you will understand the reverent worship of the Lord
and you will find the Knowledge of God.
For it is the Lord Himself who gives Knowledge —
and from His mouth come wisdom and understanding.

The Proverbs 2

The wolf stays with the lamb,

and the leopard lies down with the goat;

a calf and young lion and fatling are together;

and a little child is leader over them.

The cow and the bear feed;

their young ones lie down together:

and a lion eats straw like the ox.

The sucking child plays by the hole of a snake,

and the weaned child puts his hand

on the dragon's den.

They do no evil nor destroy in all my holy mountain:

for the earth has been full with the Knowledge of God,

as the waters cover the sea.

Isaiah 11

As a deer pants for running brooks,

in the same way, my soul pants for you, O God.

My soul thirsts for God, for the living God.

When do I enter in and see the face of God?

Psalm 42

The disciples asked,

> *Why do you speak to the people in parables?*

Jesus replied,

> *The Knowledge of the secrets of the kingdom of heaven*
> *has been given to you, but not to them.*
> *Whoever has, will be given more,*
> *and he will have an abundance.*
> *Whoever does not have,*
> *even what he has will be taken from him.*
> *This is why I speak to them in parables.*
> *Though seeing, they do not see;*
> *though hearing, they do not hear or understand.*
> *People's hearts have become calloused;*
> *they hardly hear with their ears,*
> *and they have closed their eyes.*
> *Otherwise they might see with their eyes,*
> *hear with their ears, understand with their hearts*
> *and turn, and I would heal them.*
> *Blessed are your eyes because they see,*
> *and your ears because they hear.*
> *For I tell you the truth,*
> *many prophets and righteous men*
> *longed to see what you see but did not see it,*
> *and to hear what you hear but did not hear it.*

Matthew 13 (NIV®)

154

What do you want?
Light or darkness,
Knowledge or ignorance
are yours, but not both.
Opposites must be brought together,
not kept apart, for their separation
is only in your mind,
and they are reconciled
by union, as you are.
In union,
everything that is not real
must disappear,
for Truth is union.
As darkness disappears in light,
so ignorance fades away
when Knowledge dawns.
Perception is the medium
by which ignorance
is brought to Knowledge…
Truth is.
It can neither be lost
nor sought nor found.
It is there, wherever you are,
within you.

A Course In Miracles

155

And now God's Knowledge, changeless, certain,
pure and wholly understandable, enters its kingdom.
Gone is perception, false and true alike.
Gone is forgiveness, for its task is done.
And gone are bodies in the blazing light
upon the altar to the Son of God.
God knows it is His Own, as it is his.
And here they join, for here the face of Christ
has shone away time's final instant.
And now is the last perception of the world
without a purpose and without a cause.
For where God's memory has come at last
there is no journey, no belief in sin, no walls,
no bodies, and the grim appeal of guilt and death
is there snuffed out forever.
O my brothers,
if you only knew the peace that will envelop you
and hold you safe and pure and lovely in the Mind of God,
you could but rush to meet Him where His altar is.
Hallowed your name and His,
for they are joined here in this holy place.
Here He leans down to lift you up to Him,
out of illusions into holiness;
out of the world and to eternity;
out of all fear and given back to Love.

A Course In Miracles

156

What could God give
but Knowledge of Himself?

A Course In Miracles

Amongst men is one who wrangles about God
without Knowledge or guidance or even an illuminating book;
twisting his neck away from the way of God.
But those who have been given Knowledge
know it is the Truth from God so they can trust it
and their hearts humbly accept it.
Rest assured, God leads those who believe to a direct path.

Qur'an . The Pilgrimage

Knowledge of the heart is preferable
to knowledge learned in schools.
Knowledge of the heart lifts men up,
but worldly knowledge weighs them down —
"As a donkey carrying a pile of books."
Nevertheless, if you learn in a right spirit,
the heaviness will be removed and you will find joy.
Resist intellectual pride and you will go beyond —
to True Knowledge within.
As soon as you mount the steed of True Knowledge,
the burden will immediately fall from your back.

Rumi

*Our senses
and our endless discourses
are annihilated in the Light of
the Knowledge of our King.*

Rumi

The moon shines in my body,

but my blind eyes cannot see it.

The moon is within me, and so is the sun.

The unstruck drum of eternity

beats its rhythm within me

but my deaf ears cannot hear it.

So long as man clamors

for the I and the Mine,

his works are as naught.

When all love of the I and the Mine is dead,

then the work of the Lord is performed.

And then work has no other aim

than the getting of Knowledge.

When that comes,

then work is put away.

The flower blooms for the fruit.

When the fruit comes,

the flower withers.

The musk is in the deer,

but it sees it not within itself,

so it wanders the forest in search of it.

Kabir

Oh, my friend! —
hope for Him while you live,
know while you live,
understand while you live,
for it is in this life that deliverance abides.
If your chains are not broken while living,
how can you hope for deliverance in death?
It is an empty dream that the soul shall find God
simply because it has passed from the body.
If He is found now,
He will be found then.
If you have union now,
you shall have it hereafter.
Bathe in the Truth.
Know the Name.

Kabir

Where is the night, when the sun is shining?
If it is night, then the sun has withdrawn its light.
Where Knowledge is, can ignorance endure?

Kabir

He attains the Knowledge

of absolute greatness and health and strength

and of the essence or true nature of each

in its highest purity —

who approaches them with the mind alone.

Not allowing the intrusion of thought

or sight or any other physical sense,

but only the very light of the mind in her clearness,

he penetrates into the light of Truth in each.

He has left behind, as much as he is able,

awareness of his physical eyes and ears

and of the whole body,

which he sees only as a distraction,

hindering the soul in its experience of Knowledge.

Isn't this the sort of man who, if ever man did,

is likely to attain the Knowledge of existence?

Socrates

Philosophical minds
always love Knowledge
of a sort which shows them
the eternal nature.

Socrates

There lives the very being with
which true Knowledge is concerned;
the colorless, formless, intangible essence,
visible only to Mind, the pilot of the soul.
The soul beholds justice, and temperance,
and Absolute Knowledge,
not in the form of what men call living,
but Absolute Knowledge of Absolute Life.

Socrates

There is a mystery in the universe
which our senses fail to perceive
and our mind fails to grasp —
and yet it may be realized in meditation.
Although this mystery is always present
and there is no adequate name for it,
if you concentrate your mind upon it,
your mind becomes one with it —
an endless, empty, open, inner space
that may be called the form of the formless,
the image of the imageless.
It is vast.
Stand face to face with that which has no beginning.
Follow that which has no end.
If we make our minds quiet and practice non-doing
some day we will realize our identity with the mystery.
Then we will know the Tao.

Lao Tsu

He who follows the way
does not seek completion.
Knowledge makes him complete.

Lao Tsu

Reasoning ceases and Knowledge remains.
Mental activity ceases
but experience, wisdom,
and all the fruits of our acts, endure.

Buddha

Do not believe in the strength of tradition,
even those that have been held in honor
for many generations and in many places.
Do not believe anything because many people speak of it.
Do not believe in the strength of the Sages of old times.
Do not believe that which you yourself have imagined
thinking that a god has inspired you.
Believe nothing which depends only on authority of
your master or of priests.
After investigation, believe that which
you have personally tested and found reasonable,
and which is for your good and the good of others.

Buddha

The study of the Scriptures is useless
as long as the highest Truth is unknown.
Scriptures of many words are a dense forest
which merely cause the mind to ramble.
Hence men of wisdom should earnestly set about
knowing the true nature of the Self.

Shankaracharya

The process consists of discriminating
between the eternal and the non-eternal.

Shankaracharya

When one sees eternity in things that pass away
and infinity in finite things,
then one has pure Knowledge.
But if one merely sees the diversity of things,
with their divisions and limitations,
then one has impure knowledge.

Isa Upanishads

His ears catch strains of pure celestial music
and his mind lights up
with Knowledge divine.

Guru Nanak

*Even a common man
by obtaining Knowledge
becomes a Buddha.*

Japanese Buddhist Proverb

LOVE & JOY

As the Father has loved me, so have I loved you.
Now remain in my love.
If you follow my instructions,
you will be able to stay in my love,
just as when I follow my Father's instructions,
I am able to stay in his love.
I have told you these things to let you know
you will be filled with my joy —
yes, your joy will overflow!

John 15

*Your instruction
is my everlasting inheritance.
It is the joy of my heart.*

Psalms 119

*There is no difference
between love and joy.*

A Course In Miracles

*The fruit of the Spirit is
love, joy, peace,
patience, kindness, goodness,
faithfulness, gentleness
and temperance.*

Galatians 5

*Judgment and love are opposites.
From one come
all the sorrows of the world.
But from the other comes
the peace of God Himself.*

A Course In Miracles

If I speak with the languages of men and of angels
but do not have love in my heart —
It is only brass clanging or cymbal tinkling.
And if I have the gift of prophecy
and know all secrets and have all knowledge
and even if I have the faith to move mountains
and I have not love in my heart —
I am nothing.
If I give all my goods to feed the poor
and give up my body to be burned
and have not love —
I gain nothing.
Love is patient. Love is kind.
Love does not envy, nor does it boast.
It is not arrogant, nor rude,
neither self-seeking, nor easily provoked,
and it does not blame others for evil.
Love rejoices not over wickedness.
Love rejoices with the Truth.
All things it bears, believes,
hopes — all things it endures.
Love never fails...

But where there are prophecies —

they shall fail.

Where there are tongues —

they shall cease.

Where there is knowledge —

it shall vanish away.

For in part we know and in part we prophesy,

but when perfection comes —

that which is imperfect shall end.

When I was a baby, I spoke like a baby,

thought like a baby and reasoned like a baby.

And when I became a man,

I found my childish ways were useless.

Now we see through a mirror obscurely —

then we shall see face to face.

Now I know in part...

then I shall know fully,

as also I was known.

And now these are three that remain:

faith, hope and love — these three —

and the greatest of these is love.

1 Corinthians 13

Through love, bitter things taste sweet,

bits of copper turn to gold,

pains are healing balms.

Through love, thorns become roses,

vinegar is sweet wine,

a financial reversal seems good fortune,

a prison resembles a rose garden.

Through love, a burning fire is a pleasing light,

hard stones become soft as butter,

soft wax becomes hard iron.

Through love, grief is seen as joy,

ghouls turn into angels.

bee stings are as honey,

lions are harmless as mice.

Through love, sickness is health,

wrath is as mercy.

the dead rise to life.

Through love, the king becomes a slave.

Rumi

*Happy is he
who has ceased to live for pleasure
and rests in the Truth.
His composure and tranquility
of mind are the highest bliss.*

Buddha

Held by the cords of love,

the swing of the Ocean of Joy sways to and fro;

and a mighty sound breaks forth in song.

See what a lotus blooms there without water!

and Kabir says

"My heart's bee drinks its nectar."

What a wonderful lotus it is,

that blooms at the heart

of the spinning wheel of the universe!

Only a few pure souls know of its true delight.

Music is all around it,

and there the heart partakes

of the joy of the Infinite Sea.

Kabir

In the ocean of creation,
which is the light of love,
day and night are seen as one.
Joy forever — no sorrow — no struggle!
There have I seen joy filled to the brim —
the perfection of joy.

Kabir

FREEDOM FROM FEAR

Spirit is beyond destruction.
No one can bring an end
to Spirit which is everlasting.
If any man thinks he slays,
and if another thinks he is slain,
neither knows the ways of Truth.
the Eternal in man cannot kill —
the Eternal in man cannot die.

Krishna

Fear is not in love.
Perfect love casts out all fear.
He who fears has not yet
been made perfect in love.

1 John 4

You shall know the Truth,
and the Truth shall make you free.

John 8

The law of the Spirit of life
which is in Jesus the Christ
has set me free
from the law
of sin and of death.

Romans 8

What God creates
is eternal like Himself.

A Course In Miracles

Tell me, O Swan, your ancient tale.

From what land do you come?

To what shore will you fly, O Swan?

Where do you take your rest?

And what, O Swan, do you seek?

Now! This morning, O Swan, awake,

arise and follow me!

There is a land

where doubt nor sorrow can rule,

where the terror of Death is no more,

where the woods

are abloom with spring,

and the fragrance of the Lord

is borne upon the wind.

The bee of my heart

is drinking that scent,

and desires no other joy.

Kabir

There is an unborn,
unoriginated,
uncreated,
unformed.
Were there not this unborn,
unoriginated,
uncreated,
unformed,
there would be no escape
from the world of the born,
originated,
created,
formed.
Since there is an unborn,
unoriginated,
uncreated and
unformed,
therefore is there an escape
from the born,
originated,
created,
formed.

Buddha

The body will die

and no amount of sacrifice will save it.

Where self is, Truth cannot be.

And when Truth comes,

self will disappear.

Therefore, let your mind rest in the Truth.

Put your whole will in Truth,

and let it spread.

In Truth you live forever.

The self is death and Truth is life.

The cleaving to self is a perpetual dying,

while moving in Truth is partaking of Nirvana,

which is Life Everlasting.

While there is death in self,

there is immortality in Truth.

Buddha

Weapons cannot hurt the Spirit
and fire can never burn him.
Untouched is he by drenching waters,
untouched is he by parching winds.
Beyond the power of sword and fire
beyond the powers of waters and winds,
the Spirit is everlasting, omnipresent,
never changing, ever moving, ever One.

Krishna

The body which you have now
is called the thought-body.
Since you don't have a material body
of flesh and blood,
whatever may come —
sounds, lights, or rays —
none of these three are able to harm you.
You are incapable of dying.

The Tibetan Book of the Dead

He who possesses the secret of life,

when travelling abroad,

will not flee from rhinoceros or tiger;

when entering a hostile camp,

he will not equip himself with sword or buckler.

The rhinoceros finds in him no place to insert its horn;

the tiger has nowhere to fasten its claw;

the soldier has nowhere to thrust his blade.

And why?

Because Spirit has no spot where death can enter.

Lao Tsu

PEACE OF MIND

Can you imagine what it means
to have no cares, no worries, no anxieties,
but merely to be perfectly calm and quiet all the time?
Yet that is what time is for...
to learn just that
and nothing more.

A Course In Miracles

The Lord is my shepherd — I have no lack.

In pastures of tender grass

He causes me to lie down.

To quiet waters He leads me.

He refreshes my soul.

He guides me in paths of righteousness

for His Name's sake.

Even when I walk in a deathly, dark valley,

I fear no evil, for You are with me.

Your rod and Your staff — they comfort me.

You arrange a banquet before me.

You have anointed my head with oil.

My cup is full!

Only goodness and kindness pursue me

all the days of my life.

My home is in the house of the Lord forever!

Psalm 23

God is not
the author of confusion
but of peace.

1 Corinthians 14

The peace of God
that surpasses all understanding
shall protect your hearts and thoughts.

Philippians 4

The peace of God is shining in you now,

and from your heart extends around the world.

It pauses to caress each living thing,

and leaves a blessing with it

that remains forever and forever.

The peace of God is shining in you now,

and in all living things.

Sit quietly and close your eyes.

The light within you is sufficient.

It alone has power to give the gift of sight to you.

Exclude the outer world,

and let your thoughts fly to the peace within.

They know the way.

And they point surely to their Source,

Where God the Father and the Son are One.

The peace of God is shining in me now.

Let all things shine upon me in that peace,

And let me bless them with the light in me.

A Course In Miracles

Nothing real can be threatened.

Nothing unreal exists.

Herein lies the peace of God.

A Course In Miracles

Heaven is perfectly unambiguous.

Everything is clear and bright,

and calls forth one response.

There is no darkness

and there is no contrast.

There is no variation.

There is no interruption.

There is a sense of peace so deep

that no dream in this world

has ever brought

even a dim imagining of what it is.

A Course In Miracles

When they pierce
  to His essence
    they find His peace!

Rumi

When someone can completely withdraw the senses
from the attraction of sense objects,
much as a tortoise withdraws its limbs into the shell,
then his is a serene wisdom.

Krishna

Omnipresent is the Tao.
It can be at once on the
right hand and on the left.
All things depend on it for life,
and it rejects them not.
Its task accomplished,
it takes no credit.
It loves and nourishes all things —
but it does not act as master.
It is forever free from desire.
We may call it small —
and all things return to it,
but it does not act as master.
We may call it great.
The whole world will flock to him
who holds the mighty form of Tao.
They will come and receive no hurt,
but find rest, peace, and tranquillity.

Lao Tsu

EXTRAS

HISTORICAL PERSONAGES

REFERENCES & RECOMMENDATIONS

INDEX

HISTORICAL PERSONAGES

Person . Writings	Time	Place	Tradition
Moses . Genesis	1270 BC	Egypt	Hebrews/Judaism
Krishna . Bhavagad Gita	900 BC	India	Hinduism
Upanishads – various authors	800-400	India	Hinduism
Lao Tsu . The Tao Te Ching	600 BC	Japan	Taoism
Buddha . Dhammapada	530 BC	Nepal	Buddhism
Socrates . The writings of Plato	400 BC	Greece	Western Philosophy
Jesus, the Christ . New Testament	30 AD	Nazareth	Christianity
Mohammed, the Prophet . Qur'an	632 AD	Mecca	Islam
Shankaracharya . The Crest Jewel	820 AD	India	Hinduism
Rumi . poetry	1270 AD	Persia	Islam
Kabir . poetry	1440 AD	India	Islam/Hinduism

SOURCES & SUGGESTED READING

FOR YOUR INSPIRATION

The Aquarian Gospel of Jesus the Christ: The Philosophic and Practical Basis of the Religion of the Aquarian Age of the World, Levi, 1907, DeVorss & Co, Publishers, Santa Monica, CA (See also at www.sacred-texts.com)

As The Waters Cover The Sea, Patricia Robinett, 2006, Aesculapius Press, Eugene, OR

Autobiography of a Yogi, Paramahansa Yogananda, 1946, 2006, Self-Realization Fellowship, Los Angeles, CA

The Bhagavad Gita, translator Juan Mascaro, 1962, Viking Penguin Books, New York, NY

The Bhagavad Gita : Krishna's Counsel in Time of War, translated by Barbara Stoler Miller, 1986, Bantam Classics, New York, NY

A Course In Miracles, Foundation for Inner Peace, 1975, 1992, Viking Penguin, New York, NY and Supplements to A Course In Miracles, Foundation for Inner Peace, 1976, 1996, Viking Penguin, New York, NY or the 2007 version which combines both Course and Supplements

Crest-Jewel of Discrimination, Shankara (translators Swami Prabhavananda and Christopher Isherwood), 1947, 1975, Vedanta Press, Hollywood, CA

The Essential Jesus : Original Sayings and Earliest Images, John Dominic Crossan, 1994, Castle Books, Edison, NJ

The Essential Koran : The Heart of Islam, translator Thomas Cleary, 1992, Castle Books, Edison, NJ

The Essential Rumi, translator Coleman Barks with John Moyne, 1995, Castle Books, Edison, NJ

Essential Sufism, editors James Fadiman and Robert Frager, 1997, HarperCollins Publishers, New York, NY

The Essential Tao, Lao Tsu and Chuang-Tsu, translator Thomas Cleary, 1992, Castle Books, Edison, NJ

The Gift: Poems by Hafiz the Great Sufi Master, 1999, Hafiz, translator Daniel Ladinsky, Penguin, New York, NY

The Illuminated Rumi, Rumi, translator Coleman Barks and illustrator Michael Green, 1997, Broadway Books/Doubleday Dell, New York, NY

The Kabir Book, Kabir, translator Robert Bly, 1977, Beacon Press, Boston, MA

Kabir : Ecstatic Poems, versions by Robert Bly, 2004, Beacon Press, Boston, MA

The Koran, a new translation by Thomas Cleary, 2004, Starlatch Press, Chicago, IL

The Masnavi I Ma'navi, Maulana Jalalu-'d-din Muhammad Rumi, abridged and translated by E.H. Whinfield, 1898. (also at sacred-texts.com)

The New English Bible, Oxford University Press, 1970

Peace Lagoon : Sacred Songs of The Seekers, compiled and translated by Sardarni Premka Kaur, 1971, Spiritual Community, Publications, Los Angeles, CA

Prayers of the Cosmos: Meditations on the Aramaic Words of Jesus by Neil Douglas-Klotz, 1990, Harper Collins, New York, NY

Selections from Rumi (II), translated by Edward Rehatsek, 1875, Education Society's Press, Bombay, India (also at sacred-texts.com)

Songs of Kabir, translated by Rabindranath Tagore and introduction by Evelyn Underhill, 1915, The Macmillan Company, New York, NY (also at sacred-texts.com)

The Subject Tonight Is Love, Sixty Wild and Sweet Poems of Hafiz versions by Daniel Ladainsky, 1996, Pumpkin House Press, North Myrtle Beach, SC

Tao Te Ching by Lao Tsu, Lao Tsu, translator Gia-Fu Feng and photographer Jane English, 1988, Harper & Row, New York, NY

Tao Te Ching by Lao Tsu, Lao Tsu, translator Stephen Mitchell, 1972, Vintage Books

Edition, A Division of Random House, New York, NY

The Teaching of Buddha, Bukkyo Dendo Kyokai, 1966, Tokyo, Japan

The Tibetan Book of The Dead, W.Y. Evans-Wentz, 1927, Oxford University Press, London, England, UK

The Upanishads, Juan Mascaro, 1965, Viking Penguin, New York, NY

The Upanishads, Eknath Easwaran, 1987-2007, Nilgiri Press, Tomales, CA

INFORMATION

The Book of J, translation by David Rosenberg, commentary by Howard Bloom, 1990, Grove Weidenfeld, New York, NY

A Dictionary of Religious & Spiritual Quotations, Geoffrey Parrinder, 1989, Simon & Schuster, New York, NY

The Field : The Quest for the Secret Force of the Universe, Lynn McTaggart, 2002, Harper Collins Publishers, New York, NY

The Hero with A Thousand Faces, Joseph Campbell, 1949, 1968, Princeton University Press, Princeton, NJ

The Hidden Gospel: Decoding the Spiritual Message of the Aramaic Jesus, by Neil Douglas-Klotz, 1999, Quest Books, The Theosophical Publishing House, Wheaton, IL

The Holy Bible from Ancient Eastern Manuscripts: Containing the Old and New Testaments Translated from the Peshitta, The Authorized Bible of the Church of the East, George Mamishisho Lamsa, 1933, Harper Collins Publishers, New York, NY

Idioms of the Bible Explained, George M. Lamsa, 1931, HarperCollins Publishers, San Francisco, CA

In Search of the Original Koran : The true history of the revealed text, Mondher Sfar, translated by Emilia Lanier, Prometheus Books, New York, NY

The Jesus Papers : Exposing the Greatest Cover-Up in History, Michael Baigent, 2006, HarperOne, New York, NY

Let There Be Light : The Seven Keys, Rocco A. Errico, 2001, Noohra Foundation, Santa Fe, NM

Life After Life, Raymond Moody, Jr., M.D., 1976, Bantam Doubleday Dell, New York, NY

The Light Beyond, Raymond Moody, Jr., M.D., 1988, Bantam Doubleday Dell, New York, NY

The Mysteries of Creation : The Genesis Story, Rocco A. Errico, 1993, Noohra Foundation, Santa Fe, NM

Mystics of Islam, Reynold A. Nicholson, 1989, Arkana/Penguin Books, New York, NY

The Paradigm Conspiracy : Why Our Social Systems Violate Human Potential And How We Can Change Them, Denise Breton and Christopher Largent, 1996, Hazelden, Center City, MN

Reflections on Life After Life, Raymond Moody, Jr., M.D., 1977, Stackpole Books, Mechanicsburg, PA

The Dead Sea Scrolls Deception, Michael Baigent & Richard Leigh, 1991, Summit Books, NY

The Secret Gospel, Morton Smith, 1973, The Dawn Horse Press, Clearlake, CA

The Spirituality of Gentleness : Growing Towarad Christian Wholeness, Judith C. Leichman, 1987, Harper & Row Publishers, San Francisco, CA

SQ : Connecting With Our Spiritual Intelligence, Danah Zohar and Ian Marshall, 2000, Bloomsbury Publishing, London and New York, NY

The Tibetan Book of The Dead, W.Y. Evans-Wentz, 1927, Oxford University Press, London, England, UK

Trances People Live : Healing Approaches in Quantum Psychology, Stephen Wolinsky with Margaret O. Ryan, 1991, The Bramble Company, Las Vegas, NV

The Unknown Life of Jesus Christ, Nicolas Notovitch, 1980 (also at sacred-texts.com)

Your God Is Too Small, J. B. Phillips, 1961, The Macmillan Company, New York, NY

INTERNET RESOURCES

Was The New Testament Really Written in Greek? : A Concise Compendium of the Many Internal and External Evidences of Aramaic Peshitta Primacy. This free 292-page book will show you many errors and contradictions in the Greek text, which are solved by the Aramaic. It will show you variants in the many Greek manuscript families that are explained by the Peshitta. It will show you how scribal errors in the Greek translations have led to confused beliefs, compared to crystal-clear teachings in the Aramaic. It will explain many of Jesus' idioms that have been misunderstood by those uninitiated in the Semitic languages." Raphael Lataster, 2006. See www.aramaicpeshitta.com/WastheNewTestamentReallyWritteninGreek1c.pdf

Bible Gateway is a tool for reading and researching scripture online — all in the language or translation of your choice! It provides advanced searching capabilities, which allow readers to find and compare particular passages in scripture based on keywords, phrases, or scripture reference. The Bible Gateway was first started in 1993 by Nick Hengeveld while attending Calvin College in Grand Rapids, MI. See www.BibleGateway.com

Sacred-Texts is the largest freely available archive of online books about religion, mythology, folklore and the esoteric on the Internet. The site is dedicated to religious tolerance and scholarship, and has the largest readership of any similar site on the web. This site has no particular agenda other than promoting religious tolerance and scholarship. Sacred-Texts was the brain child of John B. Hare. It began March 9th, 1999 in Santa Cruz, CA. See www.Sacred-Texts.com

Aramaic Bible is a ten-year translation project by Vic Alexander that has yielded the best translation of the original words of Eashoa Msheekha (Jesus Christ) recorded by his disciples and apostles. The writers of the Four Gospels, Acts, Letters and Revelation were all scribes that used the Ancient Aramaic language to record the New Testament Scriptures. The Ancient Aramaic language was the sacred language of the Jewish people at the time of the Messiah. Eashoa read from the Book of Isaiah in the synagogue in this language. Everything Eashoa said was in this language. This is the only comprehensive translation of the entire New Testament from the original language Eashoa spoke. Every word in it resonates with the eternal Truth that that He represents. It will be a breath of fresh air in your spiritual life. See www.v-a.com/bible/index.html

INDEX

C

D

E

Made in the USA
Charleston, SC
20 June 2012